Praise for
The Unwanted Gift

"*The Unwanted Gift* is a book designed to minister to broken and hurting hearts. It masterfully accomplishes that goal and much more. Tom Elliff bares his own heart and soul as he shares how he walked side by side with the love of his life through cancer and death. They did not ask for or desire this unwelcome intruder; but through it they saw afresh and anew God's goodness, grace and glory. I will place this book in many hands in the future."

—Daniel L. Akin
President and Professor of Preaching & Theology
Southeastern Baptist Theological Seminary

"Tom Elliff is one of this generation's great Christian statesmen. His writing is like his preaching—full of conviction and overflowing with compassion. In *The Unwanted Gift*, Elliff shares how to trust the Lord through life's greatest trials. He presents his own story of his dear wife Jeannie's struggle with cancer and brings the full complement of biblical truth to bear. This book will stir your heart as it strengthens your hope."

—Jason K. Allen, PhD
President, Midwestern Baptist Theological Seminary

"Tom Elliff's *The Unwanted Gift* is deep and inspiring as he candidly deals with the couple's most prickly thorn—his wife's terminal cancer. This book encourages all to embrace their unwanted gift or thorn as Paul did, knowing that God is still in control and will use all things for His purposes. Elliff provides guiding principles to pursue, taken from Second Corinthians 12, as we strive to be living illustrations of God's grace and faithfulness in the midst of life's most difficult trials."

—Ginny Dent Brant
Cancer survivor
Author of *Finding True Freedom*

"*The Unwanted Gift* is a dynamic love story that is more than worthy of your time to read. It will move you to tears, to questions and to answers. Mostly, this book will move you to faith—faith to believe. Regardless of who you are or what you are going through in your life, this book is for you."

—Dr. Ronnie Floyd
Senior Pastor, Cross Church
Immediate Past President, Southern Baptist Convention

"'In spite of the presence of long-term problems, God's intent is not that we merely *endure* life, but that in the deepest sense, we truly *enjoy* His presence in it.' That's the kind of truth we hear from Tom Elliff. Tom has waded in the deep waters of grief. He speaks from his own sadness, pointing us to the compassionate Savior. As one who has grieved deeply myself, I've been helped by the before, during and after telling of Tom and Jeannie's story. I'll be adding this book to my 'help for the hurting' stack."

—Tim Grissom
Author
Senior Editor, FamilyLife

"Tom Elliff has been gifted by the Lord with the ability to teach biblical truth from the experiences of life. The homegoing of his precious Jeannie was filled with lessons he would rather not have learned at this time. But, in typical 'Elliff' fashion, he has put himself aside and uses his experience to teach us all how we should handle the 'unwanted gift' that will surely come our way. Read and be encouraged!"

—Ted Kersh
Bible Teacher, Equipped by His Word

"I read this book twice in its manuscript form—once to consider my endorsement, and a second time to let its gripping truths sink into my soul. I walked with Tom and Jeannie for a portion of this journey, and seldom have I seen such faith displayed in a difficult time. This story explains their faith and will challenge you to accept God's 'gifts' as gifts, even when they hurt. All of us will need this book at some point in life."

—Chuck Lawless
Vice President of Graduate Studies and Ministry Centers
Professor of Evangelism and Missions
Southeastern Baptist Theological Seminary

"I'm not one to read a book from beginning to end in one sitting. But when you've observed two lives so clearly woven together in ministry, you are anxious to know their secret to handling the hardest challenges of life. Whether you had the privilege of knowing Tom Elliff with Jeannie by his side, or simply admire their vision of making the most of each remaining day, their shared wisdom will enlighten your path, one step at a time."

—Tammi Ledbetter
Reporter, Grand Prairie, Texas

"This inspiring story of God's all-sufficient grace throughout years of persistent suffering models for us a response of faith. Tom and Jeannie Elliff, faced with the unwanted gift of cancer, experienced that grace, and they recognized that God's power is best demonstrated in our weakness. This book is a guide and encouragement for all of us."

—Dr. Rebekah Naylor
Internationally acclaimed missionary physician

"I know Tom Elliff. I know Jeannie. I saw them live, and I attended Jeannie's memorial service. I commend to you this book, *The Unwanted Gift*, and pray that you will read it carefully and see the sufficiency of God's grace, exhibited in their lives, and how it can touch you. In this personal and powerful work, Dr. Tom Elliff shows very practical ways for God's people to deal with the problems that face them in life. Read of this dear couple's 'glorious gospel adventure together!'"

—Frank S. Page, PhD
President and Chief Executive Officer, SBC Executive
Committee

"Tom and Jeannie Elliff have etched in the portals of heaven a story of loving commitment—to each other and then, together, to the Lord Himself. One is not surprised that they would accept from a loving heavenly Father even an unwanted gift! Laugh, languish and learn—all in the reading of this brief volume!"

—Dr. Dorothy Patterson
Professor of Theology in Women's Studies
Southwestern Baptist Theological Seminary

"Jeannie and Tom Elliff have been great leaders in the Southern Baptist Convention, but they have been infinitely more than that. Perhaps most important is their model across the years for their children, grandchildren and great-grandchildren—God's intention for a Christian family. The Unwanted Gift is the story not only of that relationship but also of its temporary interruption when God chose to give the gift of taking Jeannie to her heavenly reward. This little book blessed me and ministered to my own needs as few others have. Do not miss reading this volume."

—Paige Patterson
President, Southwestern Baptist Theological Seminary
Fort Worth, Texas

"I praise God for Tom and Jeannie Elliff—for the evident joy Jeannie exemplified in her life, the everlasting joy she experienced in her death and the extraordinary joy Tom expresses in this book. No one wants to be the one to write this story, but I am so glad Tom did. As you read it, let the tears flow from your eyes. Let hope flood into your heart amidst the inevitable hurt you experience in this world."

—Dr. David Platt
President of the International Mission Board, SBC
Author of the best-selling book, *Radical*

"Tom and Jeannie Elliff have been my close friends and colleagues for many years. God has used them in significant roles of leadership and ministry. But anyone associated with them would agree that their most powerful influence was the depth of their personal walk with God and total commitment to guidance from His Word. In *The Unwanted Gift*, Elliff probes a deeper understanding of Paul's thorn in the flesh. He relates, with emotional transparency, how a prolonged battle with cancer and the loss of his lifetime partner could become the channel for experiencing God's incomprehensible grace and bring glory to Him."

—Jerry A. Rankin
President Emeritus, International Mission Board, SBC

"Over the years, I have watched Tom and Jeannie Elliff respond to one 'disaster' after another with hearts anchored in the sovereignty and goodness of God. Now, Tom draws rich insights and offers comfort for hurting hearts, from his and Jeannie's grueling, nine-year journey with cancer. The grace of God carried them through their deepest darkness. It will do the same for you and me as we receive the 'gifts' He has chosen for us."

—Nancy DeMoss Wolgemuth
Author, Teacher/Host of *Revive Our Hearts*

THE UNWANTED GIFT

THE UNWANTED GIFT

Hearing God in the Midst of Your Struggles

Tom Elliff

PUBLICATIONS

Fort Washington, PA 19034

The Unwanted Gift
Published by CLC Publications

U.S.A.
P.O. Box 1449, Fort Washington, PA 19034

UNITED KINGDOM
CLC International (UK)
Unit 5, Glendale Avenue, Sandycroft, Flintshire, CH5 2QP

Printed in the United States of America

ISBN (paperback): 978-1-61958-234-7
ISBN (e-book): 978-1-61958-235-4

Unless otherwise noted, Scripture quotations are taken from the New American Standard® (NASB), Copyright © 1960, 1962, 1963, 1968, 1971, 1972, 1973, 1975, 1977, 1995 by The Lockman Foundation. Used by permission. www.Lockman.org

Italics in Scripture quotations are the emphasis of the author.

Dedicated to

Jeannie Elliff

God's perfect gift as a
wife,
mother,
grandmother,
and great-grandmother,

and whose one desire was to reflect that she was
a slave of God and of the Lord Jesus Christ.

Contents

Foreword 15

1 The *Wanted* Gifts 19

2 The *Unwanted* Gift. 33

3 Balance 45

4 Looking to the Lord . . .
  and Listening for His Voice 57

5 Enough 65

6 A Decision That Makes All the Difference. . . . 79

7 Contentment 93

Foreword

This is a book we prayed we would never have to read; yet, at the same time, it is one that every believer needs to read. *The Unwanted Gift* is a revelation from the lives of a godly couple facing adversity, crisis and suffering. We have been privileged to know the Elliffs as friends, mentors, prayer partners and heroes in the faith. As we watched them face the struggles mentioned in this book, one thing was consistent and clear: Tom and Jeannie demonstrated at every turn what it means to take God at His Word. They did not ask for this gift, but they have gifted us with the wisdom they gleaned from receiving it and trusting God in the midst of it.

Their walk of faith has not been an easy one, but this couple never lost their joy or their hope. Tom has spoken at Sherwood nearly a hundred times through the years, and they are like family to this body of believers. As a church, we prayed, listened and learned from their journey. When they were here, Jeannie would sing in the choir; and Tom would always preach on faith, prayer and the victorious Christian life. Tom has been the anchor for our ReFRESH Conference team; and Jeannie was always there to encourage, pray and love on people.

Tom and Jeannie have been used by God to remind our church, our family, and countless numbers of believers to live out what you claim to believe. We visited with them on Jeannie's last day in her earthly body. When Terri and I walked into their bedroom, the presence of the Holy Spirit was so thick you could almost breathe it in. To sit with this godly couple in those moments was one of the greatest privileges we've ever had.

We believe this is the best book written on suffering and grief since Vance Havner's *Though I Walk through the Valley*. This book will help you and those you love who may be in a valley and questioning God's plan and purpose in the pain. In the days and years to come, God is going to use this book to influence and impact tens of thousands of lives. People will love Jesus more and will understand His grace and goodness in a fresh way after reading *The Unwanted Gift*. No one wants this journey—but if we are the recipient of an unwanted gift, we should pray that we will walk in the same grace and Christlikeness in which Tom and Jeannie walked.

—Michael and Terri Catt
Sherwood Baptist Church, Albany, Georgia

OUR STORY

Just as we had done so many times before in our forty-eight years and eleven months of marriage, Jeannie and I were lying together side by side, holding hands, alone in our darkened bedroom. Jeannie's labored breathing had now become settled and quiet. I began quoting Scripture, a practice that we'd especially leaned upon during these past few months when full hearts and restless thoughts made falling asleep difficult for us both. But this time, I was speaking the words alone—first from a familiar psalm, then from Ephesians, and finally the comforting words of Christ spoken just hours before His own death.

"Do not let your heart be troubled; believe in God, believe also in Me. In my Father's house are many dwelling places; if it were not so, I would have told you; for I go to prepare a place for you" (John 14:1–2).

At those last words the presence of the Divine Bridegroom filled the room. Leaning near, He whispered, "It's time! Now, come away my love!"

Jeannie took one slow, final breath of earth's stale air, released my hand, and raced into the arms of her Savior. Marveling at the Light and fresh Presence now filling her heart, she entered this, her new home!

Moments later, I stood alone beside our bed, now occupied only by Jeannie's beautiful but vacated earthly temple, and said a tearful farewell to the love of my life, rejoicing that she was now in the arms of the One who loved her most.

This is our story—Jeannie's and mine. But this is also the story of a gift—a gift no one, not even you, really wants. By the end of the story, we pray you'll discover the reality that, hidden within this unwanted gift, are the very treasures you have always longed to possess.

But first I need to tell you about two gifts we both wanted . . . passionately!

1

The *Wanted* Gifts

*It is not good for the man to be alone; I will make him
a helper suitable for him.*

Genesis 2:18

PEOPLE LAUGH WHEN I TELL THEM that my first
conscious thought of marriage and its benefits occurred
at some point early in my third year of grade school. Life
was simple, our family was stable and our home was a
happy place. "I want to be married," I said to myself as
I observed my dad and mom, and other couples, who
seemed to cherish one another and the special relationship they shared in marriage.

That sentiment only grew stronger over the years.
Somewhere, early in my college years, I heard that it was
wise for a man to have a biblical template of the kind
of person he should seek as his wife. My template was

in Ephesians, especially chapter five, and I'd often hold that up as a model for both me and my future wife. I *wanted* the Lord to occupy the center place in my marriage, and I *wanted* my bride to *want* that as well.

One bright fall day in my senior year of college, while I was standing on the steps of the university chapel, *she* appeared . . . the one girl who matched the beautiful picture God had painted on the walls of my heart. I can distinctly remember what she was wearing—a madras blouse, blue-jeaned skirt, bobby socks, and penny loafers with bright pennies in them. Her hair was tied up in two blond ponytails, and she was wearing a perfume that I later called "Get Your Man!" (I discovered that it was actually called Ambush!)

When I saw Jeannie, I promptly forgot all those warnings about love at first sight! We had actually met formally on a previous occasion. She was a friend of my brother, was two years younger than me, and was a member of the church I attended for a few months during my last year of high school—but on that beautiful fall day I really *saw* Jeannie for the first time.

With an abundant measure of optimism, I stopped Jeannie as she approached the chapel steps and asked if I could take her out to dinner—that very night! I was just certain she'd agree! Instead, Jeannie just smiled (a smile that forever captured my heart) and told me she was flattered by the invitation but had an obligation at her church that evening with a young girls' mission organization.

"I'll just plan to be there as well," I blurted out impulsively, "and when church is over we can grab a bite to eat at the Town House Restaurant." To my absolute delight, she accepted!

So there I sat, a few rows back in the church auditorium, guarding Jeannie's purse (something I discovered would later become a lifetime assignment). I waited patiently, trying to look seriously interested while grade-school girls quoted Bible verses, sang mission songs and received awards. Throughout the program, however, my eyes were riveted on Jeannie. That's another assignment I joyfully accepted throughout our lifetime together!

Jeannie possessed an inner beauty and grace that was growing on me—and a certain "depth" that I realized could not be plumbed with casual conversation or on lighthearted dates. I began looking for every possible opportunity to be with this beautiful girl who had stolen my heart. Jeannie was serious about her faith: earnest, sincere and purehearted in her devotion. I wanted desperately to know her better, and it seemed she desired the same.

Even I was amazed at my sudden burst of creativity! With my encouragement, we began studying together in the school library. Soon we added dinner in the cafeteria as a necessary lead-up to "studying." To those activities we progressively added lunch, noonday chapel and breakfast. Finally, I suggested that we should meet before breakfast in the chapel for a time of prayer. For the life of me, I cannot remember much about the content of our praying, but I sure remember the joy I experienced kneeling beside Miss "Ambush" at the chapel's prayer rail!

You've got the picture, I'm sure. I was smitten; and, remarkably, so was Jeannie. Our love at first sight was now taking a serious turn. On a brisk night in early December, I took Jeannie to a large tree down by the Ouachita River in Arkadelphia, Arkansas. Taking Jeannie's hands in mine, and looking into those dark, hazel eyes (I always felt like I'd drown if I leaped into them), I said, "Jeannie, I love you dearly, and after a lot of prayer and searching God's Word, I believe it is God's plan for us to be husband and wife. I want to ask 'Will you marry me?'"

And, for the first time, I gave her a kiss—a sort of clumsy kiss, as I recall—and awaited her answer. To say that Jeannie was taken by surprise would be a vast understatement. Although she was caught off guard, she wasn't without an appropriate answer—an answer that took me by surprise.

"You have prayed, sought God's Word, and have His leadership to do this! I love you dearly, but I need His confirmation as well!"

This was *not* the answer I was wanting, but it was the right answer. In a daze we both returned to the campus. While I knew it was right and believed Jeannie would discover that as well, my heart longed to hear her say, "I will!"

Fortunately the wait would not be interminable. I later wrote in our wedding book, "I asked Jeannie if she would marry me on December 1, 1965." After which Jeannie wrote, "I said 'Yes!' on December 3, 1965. Afterwards we went to a play, then to a restaurant—we think (?!)."

In my study there is a life-size, wood carving of a Canada goose that Jeannie gave me on our thirty-sixth anniversary. It serves as a constant reminder to me that Jeannie also entered our marriage with God's clear instruction. Printed on the goose is this message:

> Dear Tom,
>
> In December 1965, the Lord gave me the verse Proverbs 31:12, "She does him good and not evil all the days of her life," as the promise to

marry you. Just as the Canada goose faithfully serves one mate for life, I want this goose, sitting in your study, to remind you of my promise regarding you thirty-six years ago.

ILY (I love you), Jeannie

August 20, 1966, Jeannie and I married, beginning what we often called a "glorious gospel adventure together"; an adventure marked with love, intimacy, humor, passion, tears and the sheer joy of serving the King of Kings—together.

From the outset, our lives, Jeannie's and mine, were lived "together." During the first year of our marriage, I pastored a church seventy-five miles away from the university we both attended—she as a junior, working toward a degree in elementary education, and I as a graduate student on a teaching fellowship in the history department. Living on the church field required that we drive two hours each morning and evening to school and back. So we drove—and talked.

I'll admit these newlyweds did a little smooching along the way; but mostly, we talked. We shared about our successes and our failures, our strengths and our weaknesses, our spiritual aspirations as well as our sins, our past and our future. We each eagerly allowed the other to plumb the depths of our heart. What an incredibly wonderful way to begin a marriage—a practice that just intensified throughout the ensuing years!

Jeannie and I always knew that, regardless of the issues at hand, if we could just *talk with one another* and *talk with God*, everything would be all right. Those were two gifts we both wanted and highly prized.

But there was one issue that Jeannie would bring up from time to time that did not seem to resolve itself as we talked with one another and with God. Jeannie had actually broached the subject a time or two when we were courting. We would come to a resolution of sorts, but ultimately the issue would surface again.

You see, Jeannie could not seem to gain a rock-solid certainty that she was genuinely a child of God, forgiven, indwelt by Christ and headed to heaven. At the age of seven she had "walked the aisle," saying to herself as she saw a friend go to the altar, "Well, if he can do that, so can I."

Earnestly desiring to "do everything right," Jeannie "prayed the prayer," was baptized that very evening and began practicing the devotion and Christian disciplines that would always characterize her life. Church became her second home. She was involved in choirs, youth groups, mission trips, even "surrendering her life to missions," and later becoming a leader in a mission's organization for young girls. Jeannie loved being a pastor's wife and considered the role a wonderful gift from God. But, deep inside her heart, Jeannie lacked assurance.

As we would talk freely about her lack of assurance, I would carefully explain the gospel, pray with her, and assure Jeannie that Christ always keeps His word.

Sometimes we would even go through a type of "mental gymnastics," asking if she had repented and believed in the sufficiency of Christ's atoning work on the cross and the reality and power of the resurrection, surrendering to Him in absolute faith. There was no part of the "formula" that she denied. Still, there was no assurance; and the Lord, in His mercy, continued to bring conviction to her heart.

Looking back, I'm confident that on occasion Jeannie would even pray what I have often called the "nothing prayer." That's the prayer that begs, "Lord, if I'm not saved, save me."

That kind of praying really accomplishes nothing since it is not born out of the genuine conviction that one is lost, nor does it bring the certainty of salvation. Otherwise it would not have to be repeated again and again, merely adding false hope to an already weak faith.

On Sunday, July 4, 1971, after five years as a pastor's wife, the births of our first two children and being, without question, the most gracious and godly lady you could imagine, Jeannie was born into God's family. Jeannie came into the bathroom where I was shaving and said, "Tom, I am convinced that I am not saved and that I have never truly repented of my sin, and believed in Christ alone for my salvation."

Kneeling together at the end of our bed, Jeannie poured out her heart in confession and repentance of sin. At last, Jeannie had placed her faith in Christ alone and was born into God's family. From that moment on, my wife, the most spiritual person I knew, was finally and fully convinced of her salvation. I was utterly unprepared for the quantum change that would take place in Jeannie's life.

When she was baptized at church that very Sunday evening, I noted that my wife had now become my sister in Christ. I knew the angels in heaven were rejoicing with us, but Jeannie's joy was also without measure! Her new birth spawned a voracious appetite for God's Word and a remarkable zeal for sharing the gospel with others.

Jeannie's pure joy, her appetite for the Word, and her effectiveness in introducing others to Christ, coupled with a loving spirit and a listening heart, never diminished over the years that followed. Those years saw the addition of two more children and twenty-five grandchildren to our family. With the Spirit of God at work in our lives, we began to see God's true purpose for our marriage.

We relished the privilege of being on this "glorious gospel adventure together"—an adventure that took us to three postseminary churches; an almost two-year stint on the mission field in Zimbabwe, Africa; and then seven more years serving the Lord with International Mission Board, first as senior vice president, and ultimately, as president. What a privilege to work alongside some of the world's finest people—in the churches we served, on the mission field and with the team at International Mission Board.

No life, of course, is totally without its stringent tests and severe trials, and we faced our share. We moved overseas, away from the arms of a loving church and dear family members. Then, a tragic auto accident on the African mission field left one daughter severely burned and precipitated a return stateside. We lost two homes: one by fire and another blown away by a tornado.

There were always the challenges of meeting the ongoing needs of our own growing family coupled with the constant demands of the church families we were privileged to serve. Within each of these, there were various times of testing. But Jeannie and I never considered anything we faced to be either "devastating" or "overwhelmingly hopeless" because we were confident the Lord was in control. We would just talk with the Lord—and with one another.

The Lord and one another, those were our most *wanted* gifts, and we were glad to be the recipients of both. Whatever the challenges, the presence of those two gifts seemed to settle everything.

Everything except *the unwanted gift*.

OUR STORY

It was well after midnight when Jeannie found me in the kitchen, sobbing uncontrollably, copious tears splashing down on my outstretched hands. I had started weeping while lying in bed beside Jeannie. Not wanting to awaken her, I moved to my study. But even there, I was unable to contain the volume of my sobbing.

In hopes of not disturbing Jeannie, I moved to the kitchen at the other end of the house. Even from that distance, my crying had awakened her.

You see, earlier that day, Jeannie and I had listened in stunned disbelief as our oncologist explained the presence and extent of the cancer invading her body.

At that time I had forty-four years of ministry under my belt and had already walked this path with countless others. So I knew we were in for a long journey; and I would rather take a beating all day than see Jeannie hurt for a minute—but it wasn't to be! Standing at the kitchen counter that night, I was recalling all those sweet ladies who in the past had asked pleadingly, "Pastor, will you pray for me as I start my chemo this week." I was thinking of the men and women whom I'd sought to comfort after the abrupt loss of their spouse to disease or an accident. (Even today, I'd like to gather them all together in one room, have them take off their shoes, and just get down on my knees and kiss their feet while saying, "I had no idea at the time what you were going through.") Now, it appeared quite possible that their journey would become ours as well.

To us, this unwanted gift felt like a large block of ice. It was too wet and cold to embrace, and too heavy and slippery to hold at a distance. Yet, as unwanted as it was, it was still our gift. Summoning every reserve of faith within our hearts, we realized we were being called to enroll in God's "school of grace."

But for the moment, we returned to bed, held each other tightly, talked with one another . . . and talked with God.

2

The *Unwanted* Gift

There was given me a thorn in the flesh, a messenger of Satan
to torment me.

2 Corinthians 12:7

MY MOTHER WAS FOND OF SAYING, "Be nice to everyone because everyone has problems." She was right! Everyone, including you, has either *had*, currently *has*, or *will have* problems. Sometimes, when focusing on Christ's overcoming power, we forget that He also said, "In the world you [my followers] have tribulation" (John 16:33). To those words many of us can offer a resounding, "Amen!"

This book, however, addresses a particularly narrow category of problems—those that are very painful, perplexing and aggravatingly persistent. These are the kind of problems that seem to never go away. These are consuming difficulties that drain energy, bring emotional fatigue and test your faith—problems that cannot be resolved quickly or easily. If you're not already dealing with one or more of these *unwanted* gifts, I can assure you, on the basis of God's Word, that they are headed your way. The category may be small, but the participants are universal!

I need to begin with a confession. Jeannie and I would readily admit that we were not experts in dealing with our own problems, much less those of others. We were always learning, and had enough on our own plates to keep us quite busy, thank you. Besides, every difficulty is filtered through the heart of the person actually experiencing it. The problem that is big to you may seem incredibly insignificant to another.

During times of personal crisis, you might quickly discover that your ability to articulate your particular problem often grows in inverse proportion to just how much others want to hear about it.

In fact, you may have already learned to spot the glazed look that means, "As soon as you are finished telling me about your problem, I'll tell you why I just wish I had yours instead of the really big one I've got!" Problems come in all sizes and shapes. On the surface they can appear neatly fenced in—limited within their specific financial, spiritual, physical, emotional or family parameters. But difficulties of the kind we are addressing here are usually interrelated, putting their fingers in other pies.

What might seem like a serious but simple problem on the surface can soon began to alter schedules, deplete energy, test relationships, drain emotions, raise questions about the future, spur serious thinking about your concept of God and cause you to ponder deeply the importance of your spiritual discipline. If unchecked, some problems can even create a paralyzing sense of hopelessness or despair.

You see, your problems are just that—*your* problems. And often they touch chords deep within the human heart, especially if they involve some type of ongoing suffering or the possibility of significant loss. Because the stakes are high, these are the kind of difficulties that transcend the temporal and leave you with eternity in view. That is why even the most jovial and talkative people have sometimes been known to grow strangely quiet as they contemplate what is happening and what their future holds.

How do we handle the problems that seem too large for our human grasp? Is it possible to truly hear God during these moments? Are there some winners out there from whom we can learn? And are there some guiding principles we must follow in order to deal effectively with our problems when, to be perfectly honest, we wish they would simply go away?

You will be encouraged to know that the answer to each of the questions above is *"Yes!"* Sharing that good news, in fact, is the underlying purpose of this book.

In our own desperate hour, Jeannie and I were drawn to consider the apostle Paul's struggle with what he termed his "thorn in the flesh"—that relentless, excruciating problem for which there seemed to be no promise of immediate relief. Like so many, Paul was brought face to face with his unwanted gift at a critical juncture in his otherwise remarkably energetic and enormously effective career.

Writing to the believers in Corinth, Paul challenged those who were questioning both his sincerity and his apostolic authority by reminding them of his impeccable credentials.

Paul reminded the Corinthian church that few people could boast of the spiritual heritage *he* possessed. "Are they Hebrews? So am I. Are they Israelites? So am I. Are they descendants of Abraham? So am I. Are they servants of Christ?—I speak as if insane—I more so" (2 Cor. 11:22–23).

In addition to his unquestionable heritage, Paul also wanted the Corinthian believers to realize that he had experienced a remarkable number of hardships in his endeavors to plant and minister to faithful congregations like theirs. While reading Second Corinthians 11, you can imagine a determined Paul shifting uncomfortably on his writing stool to ease the nagging pain in his ankles, caused by the frequent chafing of ill-fitting leg-irons. With his scarred arms and twisted hands, he rubs a spot in his back that has remained tender since his most recent beating. Taking the stylus in his calloused hand, Paul then dips it in ink. How ironic that he must write to the Corinthians in defense of his own integrity! But they need to be reminded of the pain he'd endured while seeking to expand and nurture the church for Christ's sake. The list of painful moments in Second Corinthians 11:23–27 is staggering.

> In far more labors
> In far more imprisonments
> Beaten times without number
> Often in danger of death
> Five times I received . . . thirty-nine lashes
> Three times I was beaten with rods
> Once I was stoned
> Three times I was shipwrecked

A night and a day I have spent in the deep
On frequent journeys
In dangers from rivers
Dangers from robbers
Dangers from my countrymen
Dangers from the Gentiles
Dangers in the city
Dangers in the wilderness
Dangers on the sea
Dangers among false brothers
Labor and hardship
Many sleepless nights
In hunger and thirst, often without food
In cold and exposure

After chronicling his heritage and his hurts, Paul then reminded the Corinthians that his heart was broken over "church" issues. "Apart from *such* external things, there is the daily pressure on me *of* concern for all the churches. Who is weak without my being weak? Who is led into sin without my intense concern?" (2 Cor. 11:28–29).

Paul was then reluctantly led to write about what he may have considered his strongest and most impressive credential—his personal experience of a heavenly vision. Paul was so cautious when writing about this vision that he framed the entire experience in the third person. "I know a man [who] . . . was caught up into Paradise and heard inexpressible words, which a man is not permitted to speak" (See 2 Cor. 12:2–4). Certainly such an experience should have given Paul the freedom to speak with authority to a doubting Corinthian church.

In the end, however, it seems that Paul was looking for more than mere authority. He was searching for some way to appeal to the hearts of those whom he loved so much. What could he pen under the Holy Spirit's inspiration that would give his voice the necessary ring of authenticity?

In a surprising answer, the Holy Spirit inspired Paul to write reverently, and with remarkable transparency, about his own *unwanted gift*. While Paul had no equal in terms of spiritual credentials, personal experience, authority and passion, there was an issue—unwanted as it was—that exposed his raw humanness. Thus Paul writes of the arrival of an incredibly intense difficulty for which there was no apparent relief. "There was given me a thorn in the flesh" (12:7). Is it possible that this "thorn" caused the believers in Corinth (and now us) to finally see Paul as "real"?

Paul emphasized that this thorn in the flesh was *given* to him. It was definitely not something he *requested!* It was an unwanted gift; so unwanted, in fact, that he implored the Lord at least three times to remove it. Yet in the end, without reservation or equivocation, Paul asserts that his thorn in the flesh was actually a blessing in its most clever disguise. *Unwanted*, yes, but still a *gift*!

So in the end, it was not Paul's heritage, hardships, heart or heavenly vision that brought influence and authenticity to his life. Instead, it was through his deep hurt—and the manner in which he contended with this unwanted gift—that Paul was transformed from "spiritual superhero" into a humble, authentic fellow pilgrim in the eyes of the doubting Corinthian church. In short, it was his pain and weakness that ultimately enabled Paul to experience his life's greatest measure of God's grace and power.

Read for yourself Paul's account of his wrestling with this unwanted gift as it is recorded in Second Corinthians 12:7–10.

> Because of the surpassing greatness of the revelations, for this reason, to keep me from exalting myself, there was given me a thorn in the flesh, a messenger of Satan to torment me—to keep me from exalting myself! Concerning this I implored the Lord three times that it might leave me. And He has said to me, "My grace is sufficient for you, for power is perfected in

weakness." Most gladly, therefore, I will rather boast about my weaknesses, so that the power of Christ may dwell in me. Therefore I am well content with weaknesses, with insults, with distresses, with persecutions, with difficulties, for Christ's sake; for when I am weak, then I am strong."

What was the nature of Paul's problem anyway? That is a fair question. Interestingly, Paul speaks of his difficulty in only the most oblique of terms. Was this a physical problem? Perhaps it is that to which Paul was referring; and, if so, it must have been relentless in its attack, like a real thorn being continually jabbed deep beneath the skin, bringing weakness, pain and distraction.

Then again, Paul's problem might have been associated with the strain of human relationships gone wrong, searing insults or distresses of the heart. And, of course, we already know of Paul's constant difficulties with religious and governmental authorities and the accompanying persecutions and imprisonments.

Paul realized, however, that much more was at stake than gaining mere physical comfort, popularity or acceptance. Paul saw that he had been thrust into a battle that must be waged on spiritual grounds, a face-off of demonic proportions with a messenger sent by the Accuser himself.

I am convinced that Paul deliberately chose to describe his difficulty without naming it. Under the Spirit's guidance, Paul was opening the door for each of us to insert our own problem into this passage.

Paul's experience can become our experience. His search for relief and understanding can become our search. And Paul's joyful discoveries can become ours as well.

Heeding Paul's example, Jeannie and I sought to follow Paul's practice of searching for the heart of God through earnest prayer. We were determined not to simply resign ourselves to an apparent attack from the Enemy. So we wrote our own difficulty into Paul's Spirit-inspired journal and, like Paul, began imploring the Lord for relief.

And this is how we began to grapple with our own *unwanted gift*.

OUR STORY

Challenged by Paul's experience, Jeannie and I made a determined effort to mine the truths God had for us in Second Corinthians 12:7–10. I wish I could say that we quickly mastered each principle as God revealed it to us. The unvarnished truth is that throughout the journey we were repeatedly confronted with our own weakness, sin and human frailty. Consequently, we sometimes found ourselves struggling to both believe and behave in a manner that honored Christ.

So perhaps this further word of explanation will be helpful: To "grapple" generally implies engagement in close up, face-to-face, one-on-one combat with a determined adversary. This is what Jeannie and I sensed was happening to us on so many occasions throughout our journey. Sometimes it seemed like we were in hand-to-hand combat with the Enemy who, if unchecked, could easily overwhelm us. Perhaps you feel the same about the obstacle that appears to have turned your life upside down. If so, you will be encouraged to know that "greater is He who is in you than he who is in the world" (1 John 4:4).

But, to be honest, the untimely arrival of our gift initially knocked us off-balance. We had some serious questions and were scrambling to find the answers. For the most part, we sensed God's sovereign control; we were "on our feet," so to speak, living with confidence and claiming God's promises. But, admittedly, there were other times when we felt as if we were on our backs, overpowered by an unrelenting stream of bad reports. Our normally positive and confident outlook was challenged at its core, and our hearts resonated with Paul's testimony.

The kind of problems that sometimes involve ongoing suffering, death and grief, have been the human experience ever since sinful Adam and Eve temporarily transferred this earth's title to Satan in the garden of Eden. The fact that "in Adam all die" is a sobering prospect, relieved only by the good news that follows: "In Christ all will be made alive" (1 Cor. 15:22). Christ's life, death and resurrection provide us the resources needed to grapple effectively with our own problems. Christ provides everything we need to go forward with a life that honors Him.

So in a larger sense, while this is *our* story, it is also about *you*, and how you can hear God when dealing with your own unwanted gift. Question: How can you establish and maintain spiritual balance when you feel as if you are continually being knocked off your feet?

3

Balance

Because of the surpassing greatness of the revelations, for this reason, to keep me from exalting myself, there was given me a thorn in the flesh, a messenger of Satan to torment me—to keep me from exalting myself!

2 Corinthians 12:7

THE ARRIVAL OF AN UNWANTED GIFT tends to knock us off-balance in several areas of life simultaneously. In some instances, the problem itself can quickly become the new center around which the rest of life begins to spin. People have told me that such a problem often leaves them feeling out of control, as if they are suddenly thrown into a dark tunnel, stumbling along with no end in sight.

How can we recover our balance in such a situation, and gain the assurance that we are following a divinely ordered path forward? This is a question of paramount importance.

The manner in which a person defines his or her problem speaks volumes about that person's faith and focus in life. Paul's definition of his own struggles helps illustrate that fact. Tucked away in Paul's description of his thorn in the flesh are three important acknowledgments that are worthy of consideration. Like the three legs of a stool, the following principles will help us regain balance after our lives have been knocked off-center. Notice what he says about his problem.

1. God is still in charge.

On the surface, a phrase like "there was given me a thorn in the flesh, a messenger of Satan to torment me" (2 Cor. 12:7), makes it seem as if God had abandoned Paul and left him to the wiles of Satan. But nothing could have been further from the truth!

Remember, this is the same Paul who penned Romans 8:28, with its bold affirmation that "we know that God causes all things to work together for good to those who love God, to those who are called according to *His* purpose."

And in that same epistle to the Romans, Paul asks the rhetorical question in 8:35, "Who will separate us from the love of Christ?" to which all of creation will one day respond, *"Nothing . . . and no one!"*

Paul saw clearly that all that was happening to him (and *is* happening to us) is rooted in God's ultimate purpose for our lives. He is the one whose sovereign judgment determines whether a thorn in the flesh can be "given" in the first place, thus turning Satan and his emissaries into nothing more than messenger boys. If you think your problem has caught God by surprise, you might consider that it was God who pointed out Job to Satan and not vice versa (See Job 1:8–12).

But our problems *can* cause us to lose sight of God. I once heard of a father whose son was trapped on the second floor of their burning house.

"Jump!" shouted the father to his son who was standing near a bedroom window. "Daddy, I can't see you!" screamed the terrified boy. "But I can see you!" shouted the father, at which the boy jumped into the safety of his arms. Sometimes your problems may seem so enormous and endless that you want to scream out to God, "I can't see you!" But that does not mean that *He* cannot see *you.* That is why it is so important to reflect more on the presence of God than the problem at hand.

Upon Jeannie's initial diagnosis, seeking to be a caring spouse, I quickly set out to become an expert on the subject of breast cancer. Night after night, for over a week, I sat before a computer screen and, with glazed eyes and a dull brain, sought to read everything I could on the subject—but it was an impossible task! My spirits would soar with hope one minute and plummet into despair the next. Reliable information does play an important role when facing any situation; but Jeannie and I soon realized that the primary key in dealing with her diagnosis would be found in *knowing God*. The more we knew of *Him*, the easier it would be to see our unwanted gift in its proper perspective.

So we set about to do just that—to become more intimately acquainted with God. That became our ultimate goal. After all, He was still in charge. We wanted to emulate Paul's magnificent obsession. We wanted to "know Him and the power of His resurrection and the fellowship of His sufferings, being conformed to His death; in order that [we might] attain to the resurrection from the dead" (Phil. 3:10–11). For the first time in our experience, the "fellowship of His sufferings" began to take on a fresh significance.

2. Satan is not in charge.

As I have already stated, and as clearly illustrated in the book of Job, Satan and his emissaries are, in one sense, mere messenger boys. They are unable to deliver at all without God's sovereign disposition. That is a hard truth for many people to wrap their minds around, even for some devoted Christians. Yet Paul affirms that, as debilitating and discouraging as his own problem was, this "messenger of Satan" was in fact given for a greater purpose—one that would result in the maturing of his own humility and faith, resulting in God's greater glory and honor.

When our concept of God is too small, it is also quite likely that our concept of Satan will be similarly twisted or skewed. C.S. Lewis reminds us in his classic, *Mere Christianity*, that we do *not* have two equally powerful cosmic forces wrestling over which one will have control of this universe. God alone is sovereign—not Satan. This understanding becomes increasingly important as we grapple with our problem, wrestling against the forces of Satan which seek to discourage, demoralize and even destroy all God has for us, urging us to raise a white flag of surrender.

In Eden, temporary title to this world was surrendered to Satan when Adam deliberately sinned. Jesus Himself referred to Satan as the prince, or ruler, of this world (see John 12:31; 14:30). But on Calvary, Jesus paid in full the world's "sin debt" with His own death, as attested by His subsequent resurrection (see 1 Pet. 3:18). Now, Satan's days are numbered, and ultimately, he will be cast into hell forever (see Rev. 20:10).

In the meantime, Satan seeks to bring as much dishonor to Christ as he can. Getting God's children to rivet their attention on a problem, rather than on the providence of God, is one of his most effective ploys. When our Sovereign's presence is minimized and Satan's power is maximized, *that* is sweet victory in the Accuser's eyes.

Ours is not merely a battle along the lines of flesh and blood, but a war waged on a spiritual battleground as well. Being spiritually prepared to grapple with problems requires the constant adornment and utilization of the "armor of God" to which Paul refers in Ephesians 6:10–20. Only in this manner can we "stand firm against the schemes of the devil" (6:11).

Therefore, it is important for us to be constantly aware that Satan's defeat is ensured by Christ's atoning work on the cross and by His subsequent resurrection from the grave. Those epochal events in history are solemn reminders to both the believer and Satan that he is not in charge.

3. God is working through our problems to achieve His intended purpose.

In this book, we refer specifically to the kind of problems that are most often accompanied by some form of long term suffering—whether it be spiritual, emotional, physical, or all of the above simultaneously. But suffering itself is often accompanied by these logical questions: Why? What good end could a loving Lord possibly achieve through this suffering? Why does someone who loves the Lord suffer harshly when so many who reject Him seem free of such an experience?

It is only an immature and uninformed faith that sees suffering as punishment. After all, Christ took *all* the punishment for our sin upon Himself on the cross "so that we might become the righteousness of God in Him" (2 Cor. 5:21). A mature faith, however, will acknowledge that what is suffering to the world is actually a discipline that enables the believer to share in Christ's holiness and ultimately yield the "peaceful fruit of righteousness" (see Heb. 12:3–11). This is the reason we are encouraged to consider it joy when we encounter trials, for "the testing of [our] faith produces endurance." And this is why we are encouraged to "let endurance have *its* perfect result, so that [we] may be perfect and complete, lacking in nothing" (James 1:3–4).

Suffering does have its virtues after all. Elisabeth Elliot, whose first husband, Jim, was speared to death while seeking to share the gospel with the Auca tribe, was fond of reminding her readers and her *Gateway to Joy* radio show listeners that it is "not for nothing" that we suffer.

One hundred years earlier, famous Scottish author, poet and minister George MacDonald reminded his readers that:

> No words can express how much the world owes to sorrow. Most of the psalms were born in the wilderness. Most of the epistles were written in a prison. The greatest thoughts of the greatest thinkers have all passed through fire. . . . [So] take comfort, afflicted Christian! When God is about to make preeminent use of a person, He puts them in the fire.

Our suffering, then, is not the result of divine carelessness, or a moment of inattentiveness on the part of a distracted master. Nor is our suffering the result of capriciousness on God's part.

It is instead, carefully wrought out in the heart of God and designed to fulfill our loving Sovereign's highest ambitions—His glory and our good. Our problems are intended to be the platform upon which God reveals how powerfully He provides for His own children. Paul's thorn in the flesh was not without purpose. Paul, in fact, made it abundantly clear that there was a reasonable underpinning beneath his difficulties. In his instance, God was further increasing Paul's usefulness by holding him back from self-exaltation, a natural tendency for someone who had received such unique revelations from God, but a fatal flaw for anyone desiring effective service.

Through all of his difficulties, the intense and prayerful battle to overcome them, the plea for release, and even in the ultimate "No!" from God, Paul saw his Master working according to a divine plan—a plan that would be for both Paul's good and God's glory.

And the same is true for you! Admittedly, you may not see that purpose initially, but you can be assured that it is there nonetheless. It was many years before Joseph could say to his brothers, "As for you, you meant evil against me, *but* God meant it for good" (Gen. 50:20).

And many of those years had not been easy! "They afflicted his feet with fetters, / He himself was laid in irons; / Until the time that his word came to pass, / The word of the LORD tested him" (Ps. 105:18–19). It took time, but Joseph saw God at work through even the worst of his difficulties. It is important for us to remember that our painful, perplexing and persistent problems have great purpose embedded in them. We should remember that it is neither foolish, nor a sin, to ask God, "Why?"

While hanging on the cross, our Lord asked that question of His Father. Of course, God is under no obligation to answer. But if we do come to understand something of our suffering's purpose, then we can reach up, take God's hand and aggressively cooperate with Him. That is how Paul responded to his own unwanted gift.

Aggressive cooperation with God! Jeannie and I knew this would be the secret to coping with *our* gift.

OUR STORY

God definitely had our attention. Jeannie and I have always believed that the plans of God are revealed to the people of God by His Spirit and through His Word. On numerous occasions in the past, we had been driven to our knees and into God's Word where we found the kind of clear direction that moved us toward a solution. Now we found ourselves again looking to the Lord and listening for His voice—but with an even greater intensity.

Looking to the Lord and listening for His voice are not intended to be mere dutiful occupations, or tedious disciplines. Instead, they signal a divinely oriented preoccupation drawing our heart toward Him throughout the day and night. Painful, perplexing and persistent problems have a way of calling us to that kind of continual seeking of God's presence.

Jeannie and I continued to grow in our understanding that prayer was our life, and God's Word our daily bread.

While that was not a bad outcome in itself, there still remained the gnawing reality that our painful, perplexing problem was also persistent. In spite of our best efforts, after long strings of happy, victorious days—and sometimes years—we would be jarred awake with fresh news that the battle was still raging elsewhere in her body. While I appreciated what was happening in our hearts on a spiritual level, I still hated what was happening in Jeannie's body. I was hoping that we'd soon learn whatever it was that God wanted to teach us. Then, or so I thought, God would deliver us from the problem and Jeannie would be healed. That does happen, you know, as I had witnessed on more than one occasion, so why not for us?

God, however, had another plan—one that was far better, though painful, perplexing and persistent; a plan that would be discovered only as we looked to the Lord and listened for His voice.

4

Looking to the Lord ... and Listening for His Voice

Concerning this [thorn in the flesh] I implored the Lord three
times that it might leave me. And He has said to me ...

2 Corinthians 12:8–9

WHY ARE WE AFRAID to express to God what is
truly on our hearts? After all, He already knows the
truth. Through God's Word the Holy Spirit lays bare
"the thoughts and intentions of the heart" (Heb. 4:12).
So why not just let the truth spill out as you seek God
regarding your own painful, perplexing and persistent
problem?

Perhaps we are convinced that, as noble an exercise
as it might be, prayer does not *really* matter. After all,
if God already knows our needs, why make the extra
effort to tell Him? And since He knows our thoughts,

why must we deliberately construct and express them in the form of a mental or verbalized prayer?

It is an error to believe that Jesus' statement, "your Father knows what you need before you ask Him" (Matt. 6:8), precludes the necessity of conscious, thoughtful prayer. The following verse, in fact, finds Him saying, "Pray, then, in this way" (6:9). True prayer, whether expressed mentally or verbally, is a consciously constructed approach to God with a deliberate aim in mind. That is the way Paul approached the Lord regarding His thorn in the flesh. "I implored the Lord that it might leave me!"

Paul did not *want* his thorn in the flesh. Its very presence was torment for him, the unrelenting hounding of his satanic antagonist. Paul's struggle was debilitating, discomforting, and always present. Therefore, it comes as no surprise that on at least three occasions, Paul implored the Lord to arrange a release. However, the fact that Paul did not receive the results he originally desired does not mean that his approach through prayer was wrong or misguided.

Looking to the Lord, Paul literally threw himself into fervent prayer. Use of the word translated "implore" (or "besought") elsewhere in the New Testament indicates that this was serious, sustained, draining and, most likely, *loud* praying. It is a word often used to describe those who, like afflicted beggars, were crying out to Jesus for help.

While our praying should have a deliberate intent in mind, the ultimate purpose of prayer is not simply to get what *we* desire but to get what *God* desires for us. Is that not the best outcome after all? People are often confused about this role in prayer, but the Lord clearly modeled it for us, teaching us to pray, "Your kingdom come. / Your will be done, / On earth as it is in heaven" (Matt. 6:10). Therein rests an important distinction.

Paul's desperate praying leads us to believe that he was shaken by God's initial, and then ultimate, response to his petition. But Paul was probably not as shaken as we are when reading about it. "What? You mean God did not grant the desire of a giant in prayer?" Of course, if we live under the delusion that the purpose of prayer is to get what we want, then we must conclude that Paul's praying failed! But did it?

Have you noticed that when people *do* get what they want in answer to prayer they are often quick to ascribe their success either to their faith or their formula? But this hard passage requires thoughtful consideration. It teaches us that God has deeper purposes than we imagine. If we think prayer is only about getting what we want, then we might soon quit on God rather than draw closer to Him.

Fortunately, Paul was aware of this distinction—and in the end he received something much greater than what he requested. Paul knew the key to praying effectively is for us to reach the point in prayer where we truly want what God wants for us.

This principle is echoed in First John 5:14–15. "This is the confidence which we have before Him, that, if we ask anything according to [in line with] His will, He hears us. And if we know that He hears us *in* whatever we ask, we know that we have the requests which we have asked from Him."

I have reiterated this truth because we need to grasp it firmly if we are to pray effectively. The only other option is to whine or pout when we do not get our way, and then cast about for another formula—and there are plenty out there!

But how can we pray "according to" or "in line with" God's will for our lives? Paul is quick to remind us that there is a *listening* side to prayer as well as a *looking* side. "And He has said to me . . . ," Paul continues in First Corinthians 12:9. If *imploring* (or *looking* for the Lord) refers to an activity that can literally drain a person's energies (and perhaps their vocal chords), then *listening* is quite the opposite. Imploring, in Paul's case, might be considered the loud side of prayer (if indeed you verbalize it), while listening is a quiet focus on the very Word of God.

Unfortunately many never seriously consider that there is indeed a listening side to prayer. But how can we learn to pray in a manner that is according to God's will if we do not listen attentively to what He is saying? As I have written previously, we should all reflect seriously on the truth that the plans of God are revealed to the man or woman of God by the Spirit of God and through the Word of God.

Paul emphasized this truth when writing Timothy: "All Scripture is inspired by God and profitable for teaching, for reproof, for correction, for training in righteousness, so that the man of God may be adequate, equipped for every good work" (2 Tim. 3:16–17). Prayer is a good work that requires the kind of equipping associated with faithful attention to the Word of God.

Saturating our hearts with the consistent, studied reading of God's Word brings focus, understanding and effectiveness to the activity of praying. This practice enables us to frame our prayers within the parameters of what He has revealed as His will for our lives.

Then, in prayer, we can subordinate our own stubborn and restless will to that of our perfect and loving heavenly Father. Bit by bit, our praying then comes to reflect our awareness and understanding of His sovereign purpose for our lives.

One of my mentors, E.F. "Preacher" Hallock, was fond of reminding us that prayer and the study of God's Word are like the two wings of an airplane. This was his way of emphasizing that both *looking* to the Lord and *listening* for His voice are essential elements of effective prayer!

Paul listened, the Lord spoke, and Paul received the revelation of God's will with remarkable gratitude (see 2 Cor. 12:9–10). What appeared to be a devastating refusal on God's part was seen in the light of its greater good, embraced by Paul, and adopted as a reminder of God's constant grace . . . thus becoming the abiding spiritual fragrance that characterized Paul's life.

As Paul looked for the Lord and listened to Him, His unwanted gift was transformed into a platform upon which God would display His unfathomable grace.

OUR STORY

Puzzling, agonizing, distracting . . . these words and more like them described the problem Jeannie and I were facing. And ours was only a battle with cancer! There are many people facing even greater difficulties. Perhaps you are one of those people, even now wondering if victory will ever be possible. And if so, what will that "victory" look like?

"Battling cancer!" That's how so many people described our situation, unaware that there were many other issues confronting us in addition to the actual cancer itself. As I mentioned earlier, painful, perplexing and persistent problems usually put their fingers in other pies as well. Cancer was merely one front on which the battle was pitched.

During this particular journey together, the Lord gave us repeated opportunities to seek Him regarding other major issues in addition to the "battle with cancer," including a change of both ministry and geographical location.

Months of grueling chemotherapy were sometimes followed by happy and busy years of freedom, during which we would rebuild our lives and schedules and refocus our vision. Then would come the "surprise" discovery of new cancer involvement and the "new normal" that accompanied it.

So much was at stake! And as Jeannie and I unceasingly implored the Lord for direction, He began to answer in a surprising fashion. Prayer *does* change things. Sometimes it does so by changing the people who pray. That is what was happening to us.

God began teaching us the joy of savoring His moment-by-moment presence—even when the larger, long-term prospect looked increasingly bleak. After all, He is with us regardless! One morning, as I closed the devotional book from which we'd been reading, Jeannie turned her gaze from the fireplace, looked into my eyes and tearfully exclaimed, "Don't you just absolutely *love* our life together?"

We prayed—and headed out the door for another round of chemo.

5

Enough

And He has said to me, "My grace is sufficient for you, for power is perfected in weakness."

2 Corinthians 12:9

WHEN I WAS JUST A SMALL BOY, our family found itself in the path of one of those fierce tornadoes for which Oklahoma is notorious. With only seconds to spare, my father gathered up my sister and me and force-fully shoved us under a bed. In the process of saving our lives, however, my dad inadvertently stuck his finger in my eye causing me to cry out in pain. What I *wanted* was relief from the pain in my eye. But what I *needed* was rescue from the fury of a storm that would leave sixty-nine people dead.

When we find ourselves in the midst of a painful problem, it is easy to lose sight of the fact that bigger issues are often in the background. Our problems, and their tendency to drive us to God, may be saving us from other calamities of unseen proportions. That was certainly the case with Paul who readily admitted that his thorn in the flesh was, in fact, a divine rescue of sorts, saving him from the fatal flaws of arrogance and self-exaltation.

In the face of troubles, it is both proper and natural to cry out to God for relief. But, as we have seen, our tendency is to gauge the effectiveness of our praying by whether we get what we want. Paul did not get what he requested! But he did receive a two-fold answer from God that was far superior to his request. God's answer for Paul included both a *fact* and an *explanation*.

The Fact

"My grace is sufficient for you," said the Lord (2 Cor. 12:9). On the surface that answer might seem a small consolation when we are crying out to the Lord for relief. But this merely reveals our limited understanding of both God's grace and its sufficiency in all things.

It is the grace of God that lifts our Christian faith above all humanly contrived religions. God's grace—His loving favor granted with absolutely no merit on our part; displayed gloriously in our Lord's life, death, burial and resurrection; and culminating in the free offer of salvation, forgiveness and eternal life to all who will repent and believe in Him—is breathtaking in its scope.

God's grace provides both the power to live today and the promise of life beyond the grave. Never once has the grace of God been tested and found wanting. Nor has the well of God's grace ever disappointed those who come to it, no matter how deeply they may drink.

God's answer to Paul's desperate prayer was the promise that, in Christ, he could be assured of the right measure of all that he needed, all the time. "My grace is sufficient for you!"

By His response to Paul's urgent appeal, God was assuring Paul of sufficient provision *and* inviting him to remain in an ongoing position of faith. There, in that position of simple faith, Paul would experience, moment by moment, the absolute sufficiency of God's grace. Paul could never exhaust the supply of God's grace any more than a fish can exhaust the supply of the ocean in which it swims—nor can you. It is easy to become so focused on the pain and discomfort of our problems that we miss the greater objectives of God behind them. Just as hunger and thirst call us to the table, so do our painful, perplexing and persistent problems call us to a life of robust, enduring trust in the Lord.

More than one person has admitted that it was not until such a time of distress that he or she finally understood the psalmist's longing: "As the deer pants for the water brooks, / So my soul pants for You, O God. / My soul thirsts for God, for the living God" (Ps. 42:1–2).

When Paul's thorn in the flesh is added to the formidable challenges previously listed in Second Corinthians 11, it becomes apparent that his great faith was not merely academic. Paul's faith was hammered out on the anvil of his own experience.

Thus, while writing from a Roman prison, Paul could confidently declare to the believers in Philippi, "God will supply all your needs according to His riches in glory in Christ Jesus" (Phil. 4:19). It is not likely that Paul developed such understanding and confidence on a cloudless day at the beach.

If, like Paul, we desire an understanding of the sufficiency of God's grace that is more than perfunctory, then, like Paul, we must discover it in the crucible of life. There, heated white-hot by our own painful, perplexing and persistent problems, the slag of easygoing faithlessness quickly rises to the surface where it can be skimmed off by confession and repentance. Then, all that remains clearly reflects the face of our Lord and the sufficiency of His grace.

As God forms us into the likeness of His son (see Rom. 8:29), it is wise to remember that school is always in session. While the drills may change, the reality is that our Master is working with an eternal purpose in mind. Joys and sorrows, challenges and victories, desperate prayers and heartfelt praise are all part of a curriculum personally tailored to teach us the sufficiency of God's grace.

In the introduction to his Gospel, John the apostle wrote of Jesus that "of His fullness we have all received, and grace upon grace" (John 1:16). Might we not assume that John had by that time graduated from the school of grace and had nothing more to learn?

Yet, in the closing years of his life, we find John describing himself as "your . . . fellow partaker in the tribulation and kingdom and perseverance *which are* in Jesus, . . . on the island called Patmos because of the word of God and the testimony of Jesus" (Rev. 1:9). John's exile—one more painful, perplexing, persistent problem—apparently provided the very environment in which God could entrust him with His breathtaking revelation of Christ and the consummation of the ages.

Interestingly, note that in the last sentence of this final book in the New Testament, John pens, "The grace of the Lord Jesus be with all. Amen" (22:21). An awareness of God's sufficient grace was still vibrant and growing in John's heart.

What the Lord was determined to show Paul, and is determined to show us as well, was the absolute sufficiency, or "enough-ness," of His grace. In Christ we receive everything needed for life, death, holiness, and a service that honors and brings glory to Him.

The difficult lesson for Paul to learn—and for us as well—is the continuing aspect of God's grace. God's grace can both solve our problems and sustain us through them. God's sustaining grace subsequently creates within us the kind of stolid, enduring faith that is associated with spiritual maturity. But how might we truly learn this until we first come to the point of needing it?

God's grace is sufficient—enough and more than enough—even in the face of our most painful, perplexing, persistent problems. It is impossible, in fact, to overstate the vast sufficiency of God's grace.

Imagine that, in your desire to comprehend the vastness of an ocean, you travel to its shores and gaze out across its endless waters. But wanting more, you climb to a nearby mountain peak that extends your ocean view by many miles. Still wanting to grasp the ocean's vastness, you then sail out into the ocean to a point from which all you can see in every direction is nothing but its waters. Returning home, you feel as if you are something of an expert on the mammoth scope of the ocean.

At least you feel that way until someone reminds you that all you've seen is the mere *top* of the ocean and that beneath its roiling surface lay mountain ranges that rival any seen on earth! Such is the reservoir of God's grace available to you!

The Explanation

The fact that God's grace is both available *to us* and more than ample *for us* in any situation gives rise to certain legitimate questions: If God's grace is sufficient, why do His children experience problems at all? Why should we ever be forced to implore Him for a solution? What kind of God enjoys watching His children grasp for His answers to prayer? For what reason would a loving Father ever deny us the relief we are seeking? Why would God, instead, seem to shrug His shoulders and say, "Live with it"?

Remarkably, God desires that we not only possess cerebral knowledge regarding the sufficiency of His grace, but that we *experience* it as well. Such experience not only matures our faith, it also increases our utility. Our lives then become the platforms from which others can view the powerful grace of God. It is for this reason that God gave Paul (and now gives us) a critical explanation associated with the dynamic operation of His grace. "My grace is sufficient for you, *for power is perfected in weakness*" (2 Cor. 12:9).

Carefully consider God's explanation when its key words are translated into their original meanings:

- *power*—strength and ability to accomplish all things
- *perfected*—carried out to its full and proper end
- *in*—by or through the means of
- *weakness*—infirmity or lack of strength

Now let's read this verse again, replacing the key words with their original meanings and, thereby, giving us a fuller understanding of what God is saying. *My strength and ability to accomplish all things is carried out to its full and proper end through the means of [your own] infirmity or lack of strength.*

Paul saw that his thorn in the flesh was God's invitation to a deeper level of faith, surrender and effectiveness. By "weakening" Paul, God was offering to remove the very thing Paul was most prone to trust—himself! Thrown into a position that required constant surrender and faith in the Lord, Paul's life would now become the stage on which God's power could be clearly viewed by both believers and unbelievers alike.

In my college years, I was privileged to pastor a small church in southern Arkansas. Each weekend I traveled the road between the college I attended and the small town where the church was located. Along that road was a bridge spanning a sizeable stream that could become quite powerful when it rained for any length of time. On one particularly rainy day, I was surprised to see that on one side of the bridge the stream was growing wider and wider, while on the other side the stream seemed quite normal. It was clear that, beneath the bridge there was a collection of debris that was blocking the stream's powerful flow.

God's message to Paul, and to us, was that He was using Paul's thorn in the flesh, and the desperate search for God associated with it, to clear out selfish debris that was blocking the mighty flow of His power. Stripped of self-exaltation and weakened by the attack, Paul's life then became the channel through which God's mighty power could flow unchecked. If Paul would make the proper adjustments, others could more clearly see God at work. And he did!

Little did Jeannie and I know that on the near horizon there would be a crushing moment of truth. Would we make the correct decisions regarding our unwanted gift?

OUR STORY

We arose early that late-summer morning, keenly aware that the day before us was of incredible significance. First there would be a visit with the oncologist, where we would receive a report from Jeannie's most recent scans. From the oncologist's office, we would immediately drive to a local church.

There we would eat dinner with dear friends, and I would then preach the funeral message for a thirty-nine-year-old wife and mother of seven children who had died of cancer. I had been her pastor for twenty years, performed her wedding to a fine young man, and rejoiced at the births and dedications of their children. Our own daughter, a close and longtime friend, would also be sharing in that service. On the surface, it promised to be a busy and emotion-packed few hours. Little did we guess what lay ahead!

Prior to entering the oncologist's office, Jeannie and I prayed again for a "good" report. For almost nine years, we had sought the best counsel and received the loving attention of Jeannie's medical team. When the cancer was first diagnosed, Jeannie had undergone surgery, radiation and chemotherapy. Then, three years later, the cancer reappeared. Further surgery and chemotherapy had resulted in remission for almost four years now. But we had been troubled by some recent indications that the cancer was back and were eager to hear the results of the regularly scheduled scan.

"The cancer has returned," said the doctor somberly. He was a fellow-believer, highly regarded in his profession and incredibly competent and compassionate. Over the years we had developed a warm friendship. "In fact," he continued, obviously downcast, "it appears the cancer has metastasized, spreading to your lungs and your liver. The best approach is immediate, aggressive chemotherapy. How soon can we start?"

How soon could we start? We had little time to process the devastating news on the short drive to the church. There, we sat together on the front row and listened to our daughter (who knew nothing of our own report) emotionally eulogize her friend.

Jeannie and I struggled to put our own painful, perplexing problem in perspective.

After all, we had been married almost fifty years, and had already watched with delight as our family had grown to four children, their spouses and twenty-five grandchildren.

We somehow felt selfish at our own sense of devastation since this was the funeral service for a dear

Christian wife and mother who never had the opportunity to see her children become adults, let alone reach the age of forty!

On the way home, Jeannie and I found it difficult to even take a deep breath as we discussed how to share the doctor's report with our own children, including our grief-stricken daughter who had just spoken at her friend's funeral.

Our big question now was not, "How *could* we move forward?" but, "How *would* we move forward?" Would Paul's experience continue to be our guide for the days ahead? Would we make the same discoveries and express the same disposition as Paul? Would we approach the next stage of our painful, perplexing and persistent problem with authentic faith and genuine joy?

With the doctor's report now laying heavily on our hearts, Jeannie and I knew we were once again being called to make an important decision: What *would* we do with our *unwanted gift*?

6

A Decision That Makes All the Difference

Most gladly, therefore, I will rather boast about my weaknesses, so that the power of Christ may dwell in me.

2 Corinthians 12:9

"CRYING IS ALL RIGHT IN ITS WAY while it lasts. But you have to stop sooner or later, and then you still have to decide what to do." So muses C.S. Lewis in *The Silver Chair*, the sixth book in his classic fantasy series *The Chronicles of Narnia*. Lewis is right! When confronted with any problem, it is imperative to make a timely decision. Unfortunately, many of us find it far too easy to park somewhere in the process, thus failing to move forward.

Earlier in our marriage, Jeannie and I had learned the importance of making timely, deliberate, Spirit-led decisions as we listened to a speaker I'd invited to share with the congregation I was then leading. Suffering since birth with cerebral palsy, the speaker, now an older man, shared his story of God's grace and provision.

Jeannie and I sat in rapt attention with the others in attendance that Sunday morning, straining to hear clearly the message delivered with slurred speech from a mouth that was both crooked and dribbling saliva.

But it was the man's heart we were hearing, and from it poured the refreshing, life-changing Word of God. Speech was too energy-consuming for him to waste time on foolish stories and meaningless meanderings.

With what strength he could muster, he verbally drew a line in the sand and called for a decision of the kind he had made so many years earlier—a decision first to trust in the Lord and then to trust God's grace for every need in life.

Our speaker's life was a simple illustration of God's power, first to *save* and then to *use* a life surrendered to Him. If anything, his painful, perplexing and persistent problems had simply cast him on the Lord in a manner those of us without his difficulties would find challenging, to say the least. That evening, as the power of God was released, unhindered, through the life of someone whose very weakness was compelling, Jeannie and I saw the value of making Spirit-led decisions that glorified God and placed us in the center of His will. Now here we were, years later, being challenged with our own distressing set of circumstances. Would we, like the speaker on that long ago night, and like Paul before him, make the right decision about the problem that had enveloped our lives?

Who wants a thorn in the flesh anyway? Certainly, neither Paul nor any of the rest of us desire the kind of problems that stay with us all day, every day.

Like Paul, we go to inordinate lengths to dodge all kinds of difficulties, especially those that seem to have no solution. Thus, marriages end in frustration, children walk out the door (physically, emotionally and spiritually), work is terminated, church members and pastors depart, friendships are severed, and some desperate people even choose to end their lives.

But Paul chose one simple path that, in the end, made all the difference. When it became obvious that there was no way to eradicate or escape from his unwanted gift, Paul decided instead to *embrace* it.

How do you embrace a painful, perplexing and persistent problem? What do you do when, in spite of all your pleading, God says, "This problem is *not* going away?"

Of course, many people simply cannot conceive that the Lord would ever say such a thing. Wallowing in their misguided understanding and puny concept of God, they either turn away from Him completely or surround themselves with well-meaning but naive friends who feel the same.

After all, if God loves them, why should He not give them what they want? Isn't that what He's there for?

But there is a different approach, the approach Paul models for us here—one that guides us to the right decision. "Most gladly, therefore, I will rather boast about my weaknesses, so that the power of Christ may dwell in me" (2 Cor. 12:9). Mind you, Paul did not simply roll over and play dead when faced with his thorn in the flesh. Instead, he rolled up his sleeves and went to work, imploring the Lord at least three times to remove his thorn in the flesh. Only heaven knows how much time Paul spent crying out in agonizing prayer, watching and then waiting for the answer.

But the answer that came must have been horribly disappointing to Paul initially. The essence of God's response was this:

> No. I will not remove this painful, perplexing and persistent problem. Instead, I will use it to provide something far better for you,

something that will demand a constant casting of yourself on Me. And as you come to Me in surrender, casting yourself on Me and trusting in My grace, a remarkable transition will take place. My power and My grace will become the most obvious attributes of your life, and they will be more visible to others than either your problem or your personality. I will give you all the power and grace you need for living a full and abundant life.

So Paul decided to reach up, take the hand of God, and aggressively cooperate with Him.

As you may recall, Paul had exhausted all the normal approaches for generating respect on the part of the Corinthian church. He had boasted of his heritage, his hurts, his heart and his heavenly vision—all *his* strengths. Now God turned Paul's attention to his previously undisclosed weakness, a thorn in the flesh from which there was no apparent relief.

In the end, Paul chose to make the one decision that made all the difference—"I will boast about my weakness!" And in that moment Paul's reliance on God took a quantum leap; the genuine nature of his faith became proportionally evident, and so did the effectiveness of his ministry. Everything changed!

To boast about or glory in one's weakness is an awkward concept for us and requires some clarification. Paul was not bragging about his infirmity, or simply using it as a ploy to gain sympathy and open doors that might otherwise remain closed. Neither was Paul in love with his pain, promoting it in some sadistic, self-pitying manner.

He was simply foregoing the natural tendency to garner attention and respect by emphasizing his strengths, and was, instead, ensuring that others were more aware of his weakness.

Few things open hearts like a genuinely humble and self-effacing approach to life, making no bones about one's limitations. The "boasting" of which Paul writes is not a prideful arrogance but a humble admission of his struggles and failures. Paul was determined to turn attention away from his strengths and to boast, or make much of the fact, that any success in life or ministry must be attributed to God's power *in spite of* his own glaring inadequacies and personal struggles.

But, in Paul's thinking, there was an even greater issue at stake within his decision to boast about his weakness. Paul knew that only by such an approach would it be possible for the power of Christ to rest upon his life. The picture of *abiding* or *dwelling*—or *rest* (as stated in the

King James Version)—is related to "pitching a tent" or "dwelling in."

Paul understood that as long as he made much of himself and his own abilities, Christ would not rest upon him in all *His* power. But if Paul, in humility and weakness, would just move aside, Christ would then use his life as a platform upon which He could display His power and glory. Paul decided to live out his earlier admonition in First Corinthians 1:26–29 that God uses the foolish, weak, base things of the world "so that no man may boast before God." God is determined to share the stage with no other!

Like Paul, we must see that our future usableness and intimacy with Christ is at stake in our response to difficulties. The question now is not whether we will encounter such problems, but how we will respond. In her classic poem "The Thorn," Martha Snell Nicholson speaks to the value of making the right decision about our own thorns.

> I stood a mendicant of God before His royal throne
>
> And begged Him for one priceless gift, which I could call my own.

I took the gift from out His hand, but as I would depart

I cried, "But Lord, this is a thorn and it has pierced my heart.

This is a strange, a hurtful gift, which Thou hast given me."

He said, "My child, I give good gifts and gave My best to thee."

I took it home and though at first the cruel thorn hurt sore,

As long years passed I learned at last to love it more and more.

I learned He never gives a thorn without this added grace,

He takes the thorn to pin aside the veil which hides His face.

Now, eight years after her initial diagnosis and treatment, Jeannie's cancer had returned and was spreading. Though we had prayed throughout those years for God to heal Jeannie, and though other surgeries and treatments over the years had been pronounced successful, we were now in indisputable possession of a thorn in the flesh—a problem for which there was no promise of immediate deliverance, or *any* deliverance, this side of death. With the doctor's encouragement and gentle supervision we made another valiant attempt to bring about a cure. Jeannie's body, however, failed to respond positively to that final round of aggressive chemotherapy.

Throughout our journey, Jeannie and I always wanted to make certain the Lord had full reign in our lives. We had prayed repeatedly for a cure and knew He could work miraculously, with or without medical intervention. We wanted nothing more than that our problem would pave the way for God's presence and power to be manifested *through* our lives and *in* our lives. That decision had been made.

But with this fresh challenge, we wondered just how that decision would affect our disposition.

OUR STORY

Unaware of just how soon Jeannie's departure might be, we sent the following to our family and friends.

Barring divine intervention, it appears that Jeannie is on a short track "home." That should not surprise you, of course, for the same is true of you and me as well. After all, it is the Father who gives our hearts permission to take their next beat. So, while we pray for just such an intervention, I think it would be good for you to know the three prayers that most often come from our hearts and lips.

First, we pray that we will remain true to our family mission statement hammered out at a retreat over three decades ago. Our mission is to be living illustrations of the faithfulness of God to every person who will take Him at His word. So, each day we ask God to hold our feet to the fire in our efforts to remain true to our mission.

Second, we pray that Christ might be glorified through all that we think, say and do. After all, isn't that the purpose each one of us has while here on earth? And that is a purpose that can be fulfilled regardless of one's circumstances. We pray that others will get an accurate and unclouded picture of our Lord as they view Him through the lens of our lives.

Third, we pray that, living or dying, we will joyfully embrace what the Lord brings to us. While not everything that comes our way has the first appearance of being from God, we are surprised at how often things that seem bad to us are actually for our good. It is only by remaining in His Word and living in surrender to the Spirit's control, that we maintain the discretion and strength to battle the things that are from the Enemy and embrace those that are from the Lord.

Does it surprise you that our first and greatest prayer right now is not for Jeannie's healing? To be sure, we have cried out to God for that! But in our desire that God might heal Jeannie and give her a few more years on this earth, we do not want to abandon what really counts. Thus the three major prayers above.

So, as you pray for Jeannie, will you join us in these three prayers? Maybe they should become yours as well.

Rejoice evermore!
Tom Elliff
2 Timothy 1:12

7

Contentment

*Therefore I am well content with weaknesses, with insults,
with distresses, with persecutions, with difficulties, for
Christ's sake; for when I am weak, then I am strong.*

2 Corinthians 12:10

NOTHING TESTS OUR THEOLOGY like a life-altering, agonizing problem that will not seem to go away. Of course, as a result of Adam's fall we all live under the sentence of death.

But painful, perplexing and persistent problems have a way of forcing us to grapple with what we firmly believe about God, His grace, our lives, and how we will steward our lives for God's glory.

Our convictions impact how we act; and—in a strange reversal of the expected—how we act directly affects how we feel.

You cannot read Paul's letters without being taken with the sheer joy that resided in his heart regardless of his life's exigencies. Though no stranger to pain, suffering and sorrow in its many forms, Paul ardently lived by his own admonition to "Rejoice in the Lord always" (Phil. 4:4; see also 1 Thess. 5:16).

Properly understood, *beliefs* are what we hold and *convictions* are what hold us. Paul's convictions, the doctrinal principles upon which he staked his life, kept him on a steady course during his life's roughest seas. Rather than wallowing in his grievous situations, Paul appears to have ridden them out with the wind in his face, joy in his heart and an eager smile.

Paul teaches us that, in spite of the presence of long-term problems, God's intent is not that we merely *endure* life, but that in the deepest sense, we truly *enjoy* His presence in it. This is one way (in addition to the fellowship of His sufferings) that we develop our greatest intimacy with Christ, becoming like Him.

Interestingly, the best path toward feeling right is acting right—acting in a faith that is solidly grounded in God's Word. As we begin doing the right things—those things that are clearly revealed as right for God's children—His grace reaches into the depths of our hearts, supernaturally affecting our disposition.

Through his personal example, Paul reveals the importance of acting on the basis of God's Word regardless of how we might feel initially. Realizing that the Lord was not going to answer his persistent pleading for the removal of his thorn in the flesh, Paul chose to do the right thing. Paul chose to embrace his weakness as both a preventive measure (eliminating self-exaltation) and a pathway over which God could graciously deliver Christ's mighty power. By "boasting" of his weakness, Paul's testimony and his usefulness increased exponentially.

But something else was happening to Paul as a result of his choice to behave in faith. Instead of restlessness and resistance, Paul's life began to reflect rest and contentment. Though faced with weaknesses, with insults, with distresses, with persecutions and with difficulties, for Christ's sake (in the line of service to Him), he could write triumphantly, "I am well content!"

Paul's assessment of his difficulties reveals a remarkable change of character. In addition to being the catalyst for the sufficient grace of God, Paul's life would become increasingly winsome, authentic and compelling. Paul's correct and surrendered response to his thorn in the flesh enabled his life to be filled with the power of Christ.

And as Christ then filled Paul's life, He began to change everything about him, replacing his old frustrations with fresh faith in God and in others. Instead of being cast down, Paul's life was now marked by a fervent intimacy with Christ and remarkable contentment in the midst of his most painful, perplexing, persistent problems.

It is worth noting that people are not usually remembered so much by the problems they have encountered, nor by the solutions they propound. Regardless of the problems they may have faced and the plans they employed, people are most often remembered for their personalities, or dispositions.

Over the years, I have spoken at a great many funerals and memorial services. I am always taken by the memories, the "remember whens," that surviving family members and friends are eager to share. But the most eloquent and touching statements regarding the deceased inevitably recall something of that individual's disposition.

"She was the most loving person on earth." "He modeled for me what it meant to forgive." "He was a man of integrity." "She was always comfortable to be around and so interested in others." "He knew how to listen to others." You get the picture.

So, as Jeannie and I faced the very real possibility of her imminent death, God urged us to seriously consider the manner in which our own decisions were affecting our own dispositions. Would we, like Paul, accept this weakness, and trust Christ to become strong in us?

And since it was not death that we feared, but dying, would we trust God's grace to be absolutely sufficient for even that hour of greatest need?

Could we be content to press forward in the battle even when the foe seemed to have the upper hand?

And would our sheer exhaustion in the battle give way to a disposition of godly contentment and genuine joy? Do you desire to be like Jesus? Really? In conforming us to the image of His Son (see Rom. 8:29), the Lord does not ignore the work that is necessary for us to both possess *and* express a Christlike disposition.

That work often takes place on the grinding wheel of painful, perplexing and persistent problems. This is the simple yet profoundly important truth Paul sought to convey. Paul decided to reach up, take the hand of God, and walk with Him through the fire of his painful, long-term problem.

That single decision so impacted Paul's disposition that he could actually write of being "well content" with the very tools God was using to make him like Christ.

And why was Paul well content with weaknesses, insults, distresses, persecutions and difficulties for Christ's sake? It was simply because, by God's grace and in Paul's greatest hour of weakness, he could experience remarkable intimacy with Christ coupled with an energizing outpouring of strength—not Paul's own strength, mind you, but the strength of God Himself.

"When I am weak, then I am strong," wrote Paul in Second Corinthians 12:10, revealing that he had made his peace with that hard and uncomfortable equation. Paul saw that his pain was simply God's invitation into greater intimacy with Christ and, consequently, greater usefulness for Him.

As recipients of God's grace, Jeannie and I had eagerly desired deeper intimacy with Christ, and we desperately needed the strength about which Paul wrote from both revelation and experience.

God's answer, you see, came to Jeannie and me in the form of an *unwanted gift*.

So now . . . the one person on earth who meant the world to me was absent from the body and present with the Lord (see 2 Cor. 5:8). I turned from the grave in which we had just placed Jeannie's earthly temple and walked slowly toward the car. Only thirty-six hours earlier Jeannie had been alive, in my arms, and whispering, *"Love you! Love you! Love you!"* Those had been her final words to me—words that I cherish even now.

Without Jeannie physically beside me, I faced the startling reality that I was now in possession of my own new painful, perplexing and persistent problem. What was I to do—even for the next few hours much less the balance of life? How could I begin to move forward? What would life be like without the one person who meant so much to me?

Deep within my heart I heard God's voice whisper the same words spoken to the apostle Paul and countless others, *"My grace is sufficient for you."* The same Lord that had led Jeannie and me through that valley where her death had been swallowed up in victory was the One who would now lead me forward.

"When I am weak, then I am strong." As Jeannie and I had walked together through the final months of her life on earth, we were privileged to witness the solid, dependable reality of Paul's remarkable declaration. Now, this was a declaration that was about to be put to the test again in my own life.

For almost half a century, I had been privileged to witness the grace of God at work in and through Jeannie. In both the daily matters of life and the calamities that would have left weaker sorts with a self-centered, whining and pitiful view of God, I had witnessed Christ alive in her!

Exquisitely gracious, soft and feminine on the surface, Jeannie's heart always beat with a strong, resolute determination to follow God. Even while the specter of death was looming large on the horizon, Jeannie had continued to grow stronger in the Lord.

Fifteen months before her death, after hearing that cancer had again begun its malicious advance through her body, Jeannie had written out her goals for the days ahead.

Titled "Joy in the Journey," her goals were gleaned from a study of Philippians she had planned to deliver to missionary ladies in sub-Saharan Africa.

I am still taken with the simplicity of these objectives and the deliberate sincerity with which she pursued them until her last hours on earth.

1. I will purpose to have a conduct worthy of the gospel (see Phil. 1:27–29).
2. I will display a selfless humility (see 2:3–8).
3. I will keep striving to know Christ (see 3:7–11).

Jeannie's goals were not related to physical healing, but to further usefulness. Should not that be the aim of every follower of Christ?

Now, I am continuing to experience the sufficiency of God's grace, and the reality that "when I am weak, then I am strong." Even as I write, my conscious sense of Christ's presence continues to grow larger than my conscious sense of Jeannie's absence. It is all a work of God's grace!

Do our unfathomable problems really provide greater intimacy with Christ and a path to greater usefulness in God's kingdom? Take a moment to thoroughly consider the opening lines of Paul's second letter to the Corinthian church. "Blessed *be* the God and Father of our Lord Jesus Christ, the Father of mercies and God of all comfort, who comforts us in all our affliction so that we will be able to comfort those who are in any affliction with the comfort with which we ourselves are comforted by God" (1:3–4). Paul is obviously writing both by spiritual revelation and out of personal experience!

Here is the appeal I eagerly desire to register in your heart: Any painful and relentless problem is definitely unwanted. But I pray that, with me, you will now embrace the fact that, in God's sovereign providence, it is also a gift . . . a gift of inestimable value!

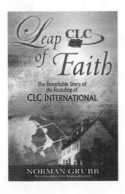

THE PATHWAY TO GOD'S PRESENCE

Tom Elliff

The Pathway to God's Presence encourages those who feel they
have lost the sense of God's presence in their lives and wish for
restoration. Examining the Old Testament account of Moses
and the children of Israel, the book highlights the distinction
between "God's provision and His presence."

Paperback
Size 4^1/4 x 7, Pages 144
ISBN (*mass market*): 978-1-61958-156-2
ISBN (*trade paper*): 978-1-61958-170-8
ISBN (*e-book*): 978-1-61958-157-9

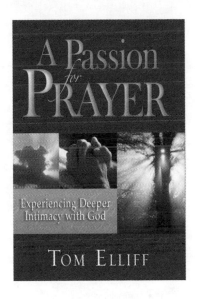

A PASSION FOR PRAYER

Tom Elliff

Of all the disciplines of the Christian life, prayer is perhaps
the most neglected. Yet Jesus' brief earthly life was permeated
with it. *A Passion for Prayer* seeks to help you develop—or
deepen—your communion with God. Drawing on personal
experience and God's Word, Pastor Tom Elliff shares principles
for daily coming before the throne of grace.

Paperback
Size 5¹/₄ x 8, Pages 252
ISBN: 978-1-936143-03-0
ISBN (*e-book*): 978-1-936143-26-9

WHEN HEAVEN IS SILENT

Ron Dunn

Gradually gaining new perspectives on suffering as he jour-
neyed toward healing, Dunn shares insights found along the
way. Moving from darkness into light, he encourages us to believe that our pain and sorrow are carried in the nail-scarred
hands of a sovereign God who purposes to bless us, even when
heaven is silent.

Paperback
Size 5¹/₄ x 8, Pages 237
ISBN: 978-0-87508-982-9
ISBN (*e-book*): 978-1-61958-074-9

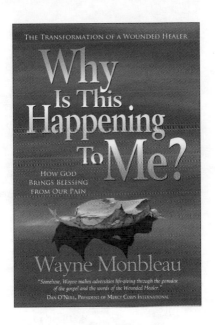

WHY IS THIS HAPPENING TO ME?

Wayne Monbleau

Addressing issues that often frustrate or discourage us, Wayne Monbleau uses stories and keen biblical insight to convey the message that God intends life to come out of death. If we allow Him, He will take our wounds and use them for healing—both for us and for others.

Paperback
Size 5¹/₄ x 8, Pages 206
ISBN: 978-0-87508-773-3
ISBN (*e-book*): 978-1-61958-125-8